FROM Couch TO College

The Fast Track to Writing

STANDOUT Admissions Essays

by Lauren Gillespie

Printed by Amazon, Inc., in the United States of America.

First printing, 2018.

www.lauren- gillespie.com

Acknowledgements

I once read an article in *Writer's Digest* magazine in which a debut author attributed the success of his book to every single thing he had written up to that point. *Everything helps*, he insisted, going on to explain that every short story, rough draft, and half-written plot idea sketched on the back of a napkin in some way contributed to what eventually became his award-winning book. 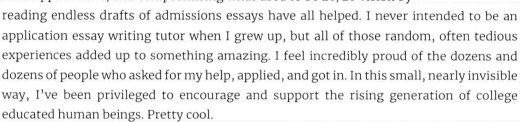 In that vein, I'd like to acknowledge that eighteen years of late night phone tutoring, helping random friends and family members with their applications, and compromising what used to be 20/20 vision by reading endless drafts of admissions essays have all helped. I never intended to be an application essay writing tutor when I grew up, but all of those random, often tedious experiences added up to something amazing. I feel incredibly proud of the dozens and dozens of people who asked for my help, applied, and got in. In this small, nearly invisible way, I've been privileged to encourage and support the rising generation of college educated human beings. Pretty cool.

Specifically, I'd like to thank Angie Panian for her design wizardry, and Elaine Quinn, Ellen Sorenson, and Frank Sorenson for their unfailing editorial support. Each of you have devoted countless hours to shaping and influencing this project, and any mistakes are mine alone. Throughout the book I draw heavily on the work, ideas, and experiences of former students, sometimes changing or adapting their writing to highlight specific principles. Thank you for your contributions to this project! I want to thank Shauna Gillespie for her impeccable taste, patient feedback, and sound business advice. Also, thank you to my big, beautiful family for your encouragement and hilarious book title ideas, and thanks to Dr. Lisa Pinto who came up with the title that stuck. Finally, the biggest thank you of all to my husband Jeremy, who was the first person I helped write his way into college, and to my four kids who will soon be writing their own essays. This is for you guys! So, study hard, get into a good school, and prepare to provide for me in my old age.

Table of Contents

Introduction

Me in my favorite hat

My husband has teased me for years that I should write a pamphlet about how to get the best grades in college with the least amount of time and effort. Whenever he says that, I immediately confiscate his remote control and Oreos, and I remind him that I worked really hard in college. Okay, possibly not as hard as every other student taking the same course load. So for those of you who are lying on the living room carpet doing snow angels while you fret about how to write a terrific admissions essay, you can relax, sit up, and take courage. I am the queen of finding shortcuts to success, and this brief, six-step guide to writing standout essays is going to take you from zero to a hundred in no time at all.

You see, by the time I'd graduated with a Master's degree in English, I'd perfected the art of asking for help. If I got stuck, I emailed the professor. When I struggled with research papers, I went to the writing center. And I sailed through Biology, Microbiology...all of the "ology" courses by doing my daily homework with the teaching assistants in the help lab. My point is that **I'm a devout advocate of cutting the fat, saving time, and going to the best possible source when learning something new.**

Given this advice, your next impulse might be to call up the admissions office at your prospective college and ask them for advice on crafting the perfect essay. But lucky for you, I already did that.

Back in 2002, when I was a graduate student teaching in the Brigham Young University English Department, I was invited to join a committee of writing instructors whose mission was to educate local high school seniors on how to write their way into the college of their choice. My role on this committee landed me some face time with "the powers that be" in the BYU Admissions Office to review their expectations, likes, dislikes and major pet peeves for admission application essays. So, while I don't officially speak for any one school, I'm offering a springboard to bring your very best game. And the reason I feel confident that these six steps work is that I've been successfully helping students write their way into the college of their choice for 18 years.

Somewhere along the way I discovered that I'm weirdly good at unraveling the mystery of writing college essays. Personal statements, scholarship application essays, business school application essays, and vocational school applications...it's all the same, and I've helped students write their way into all of them. As word got around, helping friends, family members, and my best friend's sister's girlfriend's cousin with their admissions essays gradually evolved into an unofficial side job. And reading hundreds of essays has taught me that you don't need to read a two-hundred page "How To" manual in order to write a good one.

Anyone can, with effort, produce a college admissions essay that falls somewhere between decent and amazing. It's kind of like building a model airplane. You can dump all the parts into a pile and rapidly start gluing things together and slapping paint on it in hopes that by the end it will look like an airplane. Or I can walk you through six easy steps and put you on the fast track to writing a standout essay. We're going to accomplish this as quickly and efficiently as possible, so don't panic. And don't sit glued to the couch like a deer in headlights. Rest assured that you're in good hands, because I'm like the Chuck Norris...or maybe the Yoda of writing college essays. Actually, let's scratch that image. Yoda is kind of green and weird looking, with those straggly hairs and pointy ears. Let's just say that you don't need to stress anymore because we've got this!

STEP ONE
Know the Requirements

Let's begin by picking a random topic that sounds good and writing a rough draft of your essay.

That was a test. We're not even close to a rough draft yet, so slow down, Nellie. Before you even think about picking a topic, you need to make sure you know what you're supposed to be writing. The specific goals of this section are to:

 Make a List of All the Schools You're Applying To

 Visit their Websites and Note their Due Dates

 Review Each College Application and Determine their Essay Prompts and Requirements
(like how many essays, their topics, and word count for each)

Reviewing College Essay Requirements

Before you do anything, you need to figure out where you're applying, then get on the internet and read through the essay portion of the applications. What questions are they asking you to write about? Are they short answer essays, longer essays or a combination? What are the form

requirements and due dates? It will be helpful to know the exact answers to these questions before you begin to narrow down your essay topics, because often you will have a topic or multiple topics that you could write about for lots of different essays.

For example, if you spent every summer during high school working as a swim team coach, that experience could be applicable for lots of different essay questions. *But you need to use a different topic for each essay required by an individual college*, so where is the best place to write about your swim coaching experience? If your application to the University of Kansas requires four short essays, you should only use your swim coaching experience for one of those four essays. However, if you're applying to multiple schools, you can and should tweak that swim coaching essay so that it works for all of your applications. Let me say that again. In the next chapter we're going to find the most appropriate writing topics for your essays, so if possible, find a way to recycle the topic and use it on multiple applications.

Don't panic as you read through the online essay prompts. Keep in mind that most colleges are simply trying to invent different ways of snooping into your life to find out what makes you awesome. Possible essay prompts might include: *Tell us about a difficult experience from your life and how you responded to the challenge*, or *What is something that sets you apart from other applicants*, or *Tell us about a song/piece of artwork/ movie that inspires your life*. All of these essay prompts, and the hundreds of other variations, are saying the same thing. **Impress us. Tell us something cool, or unique, or admirable about yourself. Why are you a good fit for our school?**

Also, while most colleges refer to the written, open answer part of their applications as the "essay" portion, the definition of the word essay wildly varies. You may be asked to write a small novel, or you may have to sell yourself in one measly paragraph. Again, don't get overwhelmed. The writing formula that I will outline can expand or contract to meet any word count requirement.

School:

Application Deadline:

Essay Prompts/Questions:

Length Requirement:

School:

Application Deadline:

Essay Prompts/Questions:

Length Requirement:

School:

Application Deadline:

Essay Prompts/Questions:

Length Requirement:

School:

Application Deadline:

Essay Prompts/Questions:

Length Requirement:

STEP TWO
Choose the Right Topic

It's my experience that choosing the right topic—and avoiding ineffective topics—**is the most important part of writing a great essay**. Basically, if it's midnight and you procrastinated reading this because you were watching Seinfeld reruns, just remember that George is my favorite. Also, you should probably pause and read this chapter tomorrow when you're better rested. I promise you want to be wide awake for this one. Even students who aren't naturally gifted writers will resonate with the admissions committee when they choose a terrific topic. This chapter is the longest in the book, a whopping twelve pages. So, buckle up and prepare to focus on:

✓ Figuring Out What a College Essay Topic Even Means

✓ Identifying Specific Topics to Avoid like a Fungal Infection

✓ Understanding that Everyone Has a Story to Tell

✓ Embracing the Skeletons in Your Closet

✓ Creating a List of Potential Topics

✓ Knowing What To Do if You're Still Struggling

✓ Identifying Future Career Goals that Might Influence Your Topic Choice

✓ Taking Your Time to Get it Right

What is an Essay Topic?

An essay "topic" refers to any life event, memory, experience or personal interest that you can tell a story about. And you can tell a story about almost anything!

For example, playing high school basketball is too general for an effective essay topic. But practicing four hours a day to make the basketball team, becoming captain of the team when you were the underdog, or playing despite a physical limitation... now of those examples each is a solid essay topic. So, start thinking about your life not just in terms of events, memories, experiences or interests. Think in terms of telling a good story.

Topics to Avoid

I did my freshman year of college at the *American University of Paris*, and I can rattle off a list of American girls who arrived in France and promptly chopped off their long hair and purchased more sophisticated clothing. I was definitely one of those girls. We told ourselves we were simply adopting a more urbane, Parisian vibe. In actuality, what we each wanted was to look and feel like the lead heroine in the movie *Sabrina*. It was a normal, teenage girl response to living alone in Paris. Maybe this movie was before your

time, but in *Sabrina*, Audrey Hepburn (and later Julia Ormond) established an indisputable cultural touchstone through her performance as the vulnerable young American girl whose external makeover reflects her internal maturity and budding sophistication. Basically, this movie taught entire generations of aspiring young women that if you find yourself in Paris, you should cut your hair, buy a black outfit, and poof! You've matured.

These same cultural touchstones—the comfortable safe spaces and go-to solutions—exist in connection with every college. If the young American girl in Paris unconsciously reaches for the "Sabrina Makeover," you'd better bet that the underdog writing the application essay to Notre Dame has been drinking the Rudy Kool-Aid. Those Texas girls are channeling their cowgirl boots and inner Dixie Chick like it's a knee-jerk reaction, and the aspiring Ivy Leaguers tend to cake the face of their essays with heavily underlined Plato or Jack Kerouac. And let's not forget the Mormon kids applying to the BYU schools who are prepared to leverage their sturdy pioneer heritage, spiritual Scout camp stories, and generations of blue-blooded Cougar Spirit.

It's not that these stereotypes are always true, or that they're wrong. *I too emerged from a year in Paris with shortly cropped hair and wearing only black.* The "Sabrina Makeover" kinds of cultural safety nets build bridges, and we unconsciously cling to them as a way of establishing credibility. *Hey! Paris! See my black trousers and heeled boots? See, I fit in! Hey, Harvard, I know Shakespeare's sonnets better than Shakespeare! I'm totally cerebral!*

← DON'T DO IT!

Here's the problem. While the impulse to play to our audience is both natural and valid, **it makes for terrible, awful college essays**. If you're applying to Notre Dame, how many other applications do you think invoke a Rudy kind of theme? I'm guessing the answer is A LOT. If you're applying to one of the BYU schools, how many essays do you think rely on either a spiritual or church history angle? I happen to know for a fact, the answer is way too many. A nauseating number, actually. Because what happens when you use common cultural touchstones as your essay topic is that you write, more or less, the exact same essay as hundreds, if not thousands, of other applicants.

When choosing a topic, the goal is for the person who reads your admission essay to drive home from work that evening thinking about YOUR essay out of the slush pile of sixty-seven read that day. If your essay is the one mentioned by the admissions essay reader to her spouse over dinner, or recalled during a morning walk, then we have succeeded. When I interviewed BYU's admissions committee about topics students should be writing about, they promptly responded by saying, "We can't tell students what to write about. But we can tell them what NOT to write about." **So, don't write about any topic that 867 other prospective students might write about.**

My final thought about what NOT to write about is to urge you to reread the last few paragraphs if you feel like you are special and are an exception to the rule. There

> "...the goal is for the person who reads your admission essay to drive home from work that evening thinking about YOUR essay out of the slush pile of sixty-seven read that day."

is a thriving percentage of innocent young pups who feel they are the exception and are determined to write about their special cultural connection to a specific school, regardless that it's a tedious stereotype. Please just, no. Don't do it. I'll only make the exception for direct blood descendants of famous people. If Rudy is your grandpa, you should probably write about Rudy. If Audrey Hepburn is your great aunt and took you to Paris for the first time and helped you cut your hair and purchase your first black wool coat, okay, fine. You can use your *Sabrina* story as the topic for your admissions essay to the American University of Paris. But if you can't stun the admissions committee with your celebrity pedigree, if you are not the daughter of one of the Dixie Chicks, then please, let the *University of Texas* admissions committee retain their sanity, and don't cite your inner Dixie Chick as proof of credibility.

Everyone Has a Story to Tell

After you've made a list of any and all cultural touchstones, go-to topics, or yawn-worthy stereotypes that are associated with the schools you're applying to, you're ready to make a list of potential topics. At this point my clients often nervously remind me that they're only 17, 18, 25, 36, or 59 years old. They've been really 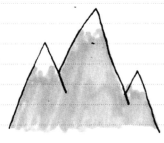 busy growing up, or being grown-ups, and they simply haven't had time to move to Morocco, climb Everest, or create the latest and greatest computer application. Don't worry! Just breathe deeply and do a few yoga poses, or a downward facing whatever. As Dolly Parton's character Truvy said in *Steel Magnolias*, **"If you can achieve**

puberty, you can achieve a past." I echo this sentiment, as I do most quotable quotes from *Steel Magnolias*. If you're old enough to apply to college, no matter what farm in Timbuktu you hail from, you can find a story and make it interesting enough to inspire dinner conversation from the admissions counselor who reads your essay.

Embracing the Skeletons in Your Closet

The process of digging through your skeleton cupboard sometimes requires delicacy. I'm sorry to be so insensitive and uncouth as to request that you roll out the dead grandmas and childhood housefires that have kept you in counseling for the past ten years, but that's exactly what I'm suggesting. And keep in mind, I did the exact same thing when I was in your shoes, applying to various colleges and later on, to graduate programs. I was never so ashamed as when I found myself actually coveting my friend's incurable skin disorder. I remember being eighteen years old and thinking, "Oh, man, a rare skin disease? Her college application essays are going to write themselves!" Perhaps not my finest moment, but such is the cruel nature of writing your way into college. You need to get real and raw. You need to choose the topics that will make really good stories and show your grit. Like, I need another bag of popcorn this story is so good.

Creating a List of Potential Topics

What are you passionate about? What do you love to do, or love to talk about? What are you known for within your inner circles? Reflect back on the stories your family tells about you at family reunions, the stories that made your psychiatrist cringe, or the story that made your best friend nearly pee himself from laughing. What about the stories that prompted your parents to increase their fire, car, or medical insurance? Can you pinpoint stories from your life that make you glow with happiness, or maybe the complete opposite? What stories make your heart hurt every time they are told?

It will be easier to come up with solid topics as you identify specific

times in your life when you have experienced strong emotions.

Strong emotions could include feeling:

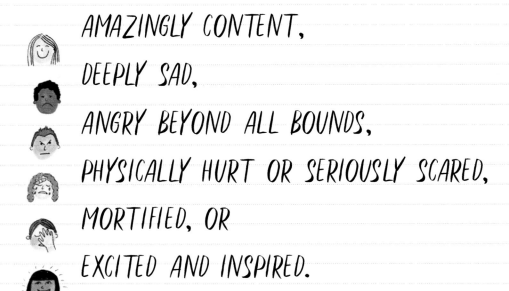

AMAZINGLY CONTENT,

DEEPLY SAD,

ANGRY BEYOND ALL BOUNDS,

PHYSICALLY HURT OR SERIOUSLY SCARED,

MORTIFIED, OR

EXCITED AND INSPIRED.

I want you to try to think of something for each of those six prompts. Ask your parents, siblings, teachers, and friends. Think across the span of your life (although the more recent the experience, the better, as it more accurately shows who you are today). Write as many responses as you possibly can to each prompt on that list. **Here are some example answers to those questions that have made wonderful essays:**

A time when you felt **amazingly content** could include family or friend traditions, past holidays, childhood memories, fulfilling personal hobbies, or special moments shared with people you deeply love. One of my former students wrote an excellent essay about a childhood memory of snuggling up with and reading Harry Potter aloud to her exhausted dad each night as he fell asleep after long hours working on-call in a hospital during medical school. Try to remember a specific moment or day when everything felt blissful.

Topics that work well for a **deeply sad** essay might include coping with yours or a family member's mental or physical illness, death and grief, moving, house fires, and divorce or family issues. I've had students write beautiful essays on all of those topics, so don't shy away from the hard things.

Anger can be an interesting topic to explore, as it often allows students to show their values and convictions. I've read many excellent essays that deal with anger, although I would make sure you choose a topic that is *personal to your life*. For example, writing about your family's experience immigrating to the United States is compelling. Writing about your political views on immigration laws isn't as effective, not to mention that you run the risk of offending the sensibilities of the admission counselor reading your essay. People generally aren't offended by personal experiences that convey anger. They're less willing to listen to social, political, or religious soap boxes.

The notable exception to this advice is if the essay prompt *invites* you to dust off your soap box. And many do! If you are asked to write about a political/social/religious subject that you feel passionately about, I still advocate using a personal story to make your point, but feel free to unleash your controversial opinions.

I've read many strong essays dealing with **physical pain**. Childhood injuries, diseases, car accidents, broken whatevers...these topics generally make good essays, because it's easy to both show your character and to make the essay exciting. Essay topics centered around a time when you were **seriously scared** have a similar effect. Teenage antics, travel incidents, and feral raccoons living in your backyard all have the potential to provide a solid springboard for a terrific college essay.

My life seems to be an unfortunate treasure trove of stories about being **seriously mortified**. Years ago, I arrived at my best friend's surprise birthday party, and, standing in the dark parking lot, I decided to quickly hitch up my dress to smooth my tights down. Right about the time I was wearing my dress around my waist like a belt, it dawned on me that the large darkened windows facing the parking lot were filled with the party guests, eagerly waiting to shout *"Surprise."* Now, that's one way to get a party started! On the surface, this embarrassing moment might seem pointless for a college essay. But what if I told you this story happened in England, where I went to high school? And what if I explained that I was the only American there that day, and

 how humiliating myself by accidentally flashing the entire surprise party was yet another opportunity for me to learn how to square my shoulders, shrug off the embarrassment, and let go of the worry that I'd be judged. Suddenly, my embarrassing story not only makes the admissions counselor smile, but it shows how I had to develop a seriously thick skin during the years I lived abroad.

What are your most embarrassing moments? Don't sugar coat it. These are your *America's Funniest Home Videos* highlights, and as you try to remember them and write them down on your list, think of the way those humiliating moments shaped your character.

Coming up with a list of **exciting** experiences from your life can be easy once you start thinking in terms of hobbies and past times. What do you like? What are you good at? What are you passionate about? Don't filter your answers. One of my most memorable student essays was about a pimple popping *YouTube* video obsession (she wanted to study dermatology), and another was about preparing for a potential zombie apocalypse (the student seriously loved all things-zombie and doomsday). Both topics were outside-the-box weird, and the subsequent essays were fun to read.

My only disclaimer here is for video gamers. I know, I know, it's a legit hobby and many of you will go on to be professional kazillionaires. But, these days, the video gamers are a dime a dozen, and the danger of writing about the same thing as eight hundred other students is simply too great. Unless you have an amazing story that no one else will write about, I suggest you pick a different hobby.

Some of the best college admissions essays have come from **inspirational experiences**. I've read essays that were a tribute to personal mentors, essays about students converting to a new religion, changing something dramatic about their health or lifestyle, or describing unique work experiences. I once tutored a guy who wrote about working a summer job as a candle-maker's apprentice. It was both a unique work experience, and it effectively highlighted his strong work ethic, as candle making requires a boatload of grit and patience. As you think about moments in your life when you were truly inspired, think of goals you have pursued, whether you succeeded or failed. Where have you traveled, and what kind of positive change or service have you contributed to this world?

Now, I realize some of you, due to run-of-the-mill teenage brain damage, have spent the past few years trying to jump off the tallest whatever or blow stuff up. Let me just say, regardless of your checkered past, I know for a fact you can get into college and do great things with your life. I once had a student who had served prison time, and he was one of the hardest workers I've ever had the privilege of teaching. Not to mention that when it comes to finding essay topics, the career trouble makers probably have the best stories of all. So, what about the time you thought it'd be a great idea to freeze a bunch of lizards in your aunt's deep freezer? Or the time you used a potato gun on your neighbor's mailbox in order to restore justice to the neighborhood? Or the time you pretended to throw up off the balcony of a movie theater and threw fake puke on the audience below...Oh, wait, that was Chunk from *The Goonies*. Anyway, when I ask about **experiences when you have been in trouble**, it doesn't have to be of epic, juvenile detention center proportions. Then again, maybe for you, that's exactly what your history looks like. If so, this is a great opportunity to show how you've matured.

The point of all of this essay topic brainstorming is to catalogue some of the best, worst, funniest, saddest and most heinous highlights from your life, and then figure out which stories show how you learned something or experienced personal growth. You might not have success in filling out ideas or memories in

> "The point of all of this essay topic brainstorming is to catalogue some of the best, worst, funniest, saddest and most heinous highlights from your life, and then figure out which stories show how you learned something or experienced personal growth."

all of the areas, but do your best so that you have a solid foundation of topics to choose from. **Most colleges require more than one essay, and choosing a wide range of topics will demonstrate a greater breadth of experience and ability.**

Still Struggling?

If you're still coming up empty, I encourage you to briefly pause your application and go outside and do something. If you truly feel your life has been so ordinary, predictable and vanilla to the point that you can't dredge up any good stories, then it's time to get out there and break your wrist learning to ride a unicycle. Okay, don't do that. But, you do need to consciously step outside of your box.

My first impulse is to tell students to volunteer in some way. The need for willing, able-bodied volunteers who want to help (for free) or learn something is endless. Ask your library about assisting in reading programs for underprivileged kids. Contact your community recreation center and ask if there are volunteer opportunities. Reach out to local church leaders or school administrations and tell them that you have the desire to enrich your life by volunteering your time and energy. I promise you, that sentence will be music to their ears. And if you follow through, something memorable will happen in your life.

If all else fails, create your own adventure. You can climb fifteen different mountains this summer, or bicycle across Kansas, or meet with your grandmother once a week to learn to crochet, or build a gazebo in your neighbor's yard, or train for a half-marathon, or read everything that William Shakespeare wrote. There is so much you can do in two months to enrich your life, just decide what you can do and do it. The amazing college essay will follow!

Future Career Goals that

Might Influence Your Topic Choice

We'll tackle writing your conclusion in a later chapter, but as you select and narrow your topics, give some thought to what that experience shows about your life. The zit-popper I mentioned was aspiring to become a dermatologist. While applying to business school, another student wrote about her first entrepreneurial business attempt. A student applying for an athletic scholarship would probably share a great moment from his athletic history. And finally, a student hoping to be a teacher and work with children might focus on a life experience interacting with children.

Sometimes your story will show a dramatic change from where you've been to where you are now. My younger brother spent years playing bass guitar in a death rock band, and his story about the moment he realized he did not want to become a fifty-year-old, washed up musician offered a unique perspective for his medical school application. Another student wrote a tender story about her Jewish father, which gave her conversion to Mormonism and subsequent desire to attend BYU a unique twist. As you study your list of topics, make sure you consider any future goals or extenuating circumstances that will make your essay unique.

Take Your Time to Get It Right

Don't try to come up with an exhaustive list of all your best topics in one sitting. Sleep on it, do it tomorrow—and the next day. Call your favorite Uncle Stanley and ask his opinion. Maybe even thumb through past journals, blog entries, or social media posts. Often, the first ten ideas are the obvious and overused ones. Give yourself a little time for the ideas to simmer, and then come back to your list and find something unique to you.

Essay Topic Ideas:

STEP THREE
Narrow Your Topic

The goal of this section is to understand all of the different "moments" you could write about for each individual topic. So, we're going to focus on:

 Narrowing Your Topic to One Specific Moment

 Ensuring that Your Story Moment Answers the Essay Prompt

Narrowing Your Topic to One Specific Moment

Here is a sample list of possible topics that a student could write about:

Senior orchestra president

Struggle to raise my grade from "C" to "A" in Geometry

Mom's kidney transplant

House fire on Christmas Eve

Moving from Colorado to Florida to Illinois during high school

Which of these topics would you choose to write about in your college essays? I hope your answer was *all of them,* because they're all based on real essays. For this example, let's focus on the topic of "House fire." If your house caught on fire when you were younger, what would you write about in your essay? Would you tell all the details about

the fire, how it started, how long it burned, how long it took to put out, what your neighbor's bathrobe looked like as they stood gawking, and the harrowing tale of your family's escape? Sounds like a long essay. What about the aftermath? How you lived in a hotel for months and had to get all new clothes and school supplies? I'm curious about those details, but it's still more of a summary of what happened after the fire.

> "The key is to avoid summarizing an entire story. Instead, try choosing one moment."

The key is to avoid summarizing an entire story. Instead, try choosing one moment.

Let's narrow down the "house fire" topic by brainstorming specific moments that you could write about:

Topic– House Fire

Possible Moments to Write a Story about:

- Evacuating a burning house on Christmas Eve
- Frantically counting heads to make sure everyone is out of the house
- Watching the firemen spray water on the burning house, knowing your stuff was destroyed
- The neighbors watching the burn in their bathrobes
- Checking into a dingy motel (with no home to return to)
- Waking up on Christmas morning with no home, no presents

Any of these moments, and probably a hundred others, would make a fantastic essay if you really focused on the details and told it as a story. But you have to narrow it down and write about only one moment because the general topic of a house fire is simply too broad. **This is where many student essays fall down. Everyone has interesting stories to tell, but if you summarize in broad details, the story becomes too common and a little boring. Instead, choose one precise "ah ha" moment that was especially poignant and meaningful to you.** And remember, this process of narrowing is crucial whether your story is a tragedy or a comedy.

Some of you may be wondering how you can write a whole essay based on one single moment? Chapter four will tackle the specifics of writing an action-packed story and chapter five will teach you how to write a thoughtful ending. But in the meantime, let's analyze a moment from the list of "House Fire" topics so that you can visualize how to grow a tiny little moment into a stand out story.

So, pretend that you're writing an essay about a house fire and you've come up with a list (see above) of possible story moments. Let's focus on the moment you woke up on Christmas morning in a hotel. What do you see? Cheap comforters and exhausted siblings crowded together in a line on the floor? What you don't see are Christmas trees, gifts, and stockings. What do you smell in that moment? The lingering scent of smoke, probably. Maybe stale cigarettes wafting from the carpet of the hotel room. Your mom has been awake all night, and your dad isn't even there as he's still at the house, picking through the remains with the firemen. You can write an entire page simply describing the small details of a single moment.

Now let's explore how that single moment affected you. How did you feel and what did it mean to your life? Maybe that was the moment you realized how much family matters and you felt profound relief that you were all safe. Or perhaps that was the moment you understood that you would be okay even without your physical home. Life goes on. Christmas morning in a hotel showed you that material stability isn't the only, or even the most important kind of stability.

The purpose of this exercise is to show how you can write about a single moment with a thousand details and you can analyze its meaning in a thousand ways. One single moment is all you need to write an amazing essay!

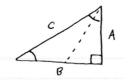

Let's try narrowing another topic from the list on page 25:

Topic - Struggle to raise my grade from "C" to "A" in Geometry

Possible Moments to Write a Story about:

- The day I failed a test and decided to take dramatic measures
- Skipping lunch to receive extra help from Geometry teacher
- Late night studying alone
- Study sessions at kitchen table with Dad

The student who wrote this essay ultimately focused on the moment of skipping lunch to get extra help from her Geometry teacher. She started the essay with details about being hungry and wishing she could catch up with friends at lunch and went on to show that she was hard core enough to sacrifice for her math grade, and the results paid off.

Both the house fire and the geometry examples show how narrowing your topic to a specific moment will enable you to write an interesting story, and then explain the significance of it, without resorting to a tedious summary.

Make Sure You're Responding to the Prompt

If your college application essay prompt asks you about a difficult trial you have endured, it's not the ideal opportunity to use the "making the final shot in a championship game" story moment. Believe me, I get it. I know you're an amazing ball player and you can't wait to tell that story. It's a great story, but you need to focus on something difficult in your life. You're welcome to think outside the box. The difficult trial could be the loss of an important friendship, financial devastation, a negative experience with racism, or a physical limitation. You can choose any trial from your life, so long as you relate the story of the trial in an honest and interesting way. But make sure that you are answering the question posed in the essay prompt.

Essay Topic:

Specific Moments:

Essay Topic:

Specific Moments:

Essay Topic:

Specific Moments:

Essay Topic:

Specific Moments:

STEP FOUR

The Rough Draft

Take a pizza break if you need to, but don't go crazy. Feeling pizza sick after six slices isn't going to help you write your rough draft. The things that will help you, include:

✓ Avoiding Biographical Summaries

✓ Understanding What it Means to Start in the Action

✓ Reviewing Examples of Essays that Start in the Action

✓ Developing the Middle Part of Your Essay?

✓ Writing Your Rough Draft

Avoid Biographical Summaries

When I was teaching high school workshops on how to write your way into college, I cannot count how many essays began with some variation of, "My name is Tim, I'm 5'11" and I like football and playing video games." That is not an essay. That is a terribly boring introduction, and I had to bite my tongue from telling Tim that he's never going to get a date, a job, make a new friend, or get into college with that opening. Equally cringe-

 worthy were the girls who wrote something like, "Hi, I'm Tina and I have black hair (dyed) and three sisters." Oh, Tina. Girl, your dyed hair has nothing to do with getting into college, and the ONLY reason that they'd care a twig about your three sisters is if they nearly drowned while swimming across the Panama Canal and you happened to save them with your unparalleled cat-like speed and reflexes. Maybe then the admissions committee could bring themselves to care about your sisters, but definitely not the dyed black hair. So, focus. You're not giving a mini-bio for your Tinder account. **You're telling a story.**

Start in the Action

Open a blank document on your computer and now close your eyes and think of the story moment you have chosen. If you want to play *The Sound of Music* sound track in the background just to make sure you and the hills are both alive, so be it. Now, I want you to write out your story moment just like you'd tell a friend over the phone. This isn't just any friend; this is your friend who subscribes to *People Magazine* and cannot get enough juice. Make it exciting and dramatic. Give details. Write it in a way that will help your friend picture the situation.

The following examples show how you could start in the action if you were writing about falling out of a tree and breaking both wrists. Keep in mind, these examples are all possibilities for the first line of the essay:

> *Even though the branch was more than fifteen feet up, it didn't feel that high until I began to fall.*

> *I'd spent my childhood carting toys, books, and binoculars up to my favorite spot in the tree and it never once felt dangerous until the moment I fell.*

> *The day I fell out of the tree marked the beginning of my new life, a life filled with I.V.'s, hospital gowns, and day time television.*

The best way to write a rough draft of your essay is to launch right in to your story. Don't tell your personal history or introduce yourself. Make it colorful. Dangle the bait. Start the story by falling out of a tree!

More Examples of Starting in the Action

In the following example, one of my students begins with a rare medical diagnosis:

> *Growing up, I was always told, like every other child, that I was special, one in a million. When I was 8 years old, I learned that I am special, but not one in a million. I am one in 25,000 diagnosed with Pseudoxanthoma Elasticum.*

This essay is the perfect "slowing down to gawk at an accident" scenario, which is great because admissions committees love to gawk. It's interesting. It's entertaining. And it's a load better than reading about someone's hair color. Here are some more kick-started essays that drop straight into the action, forcing the admissions committee to keep reading out of morbid curiosity:

> *I spent the entire summer before I turned fifteen sitting next to my grandmother, rubbing the purple veins on her hands, and wondering each day if today was THE day.*

> *Growing up in a wealthy suburb, I thought we were poor. And then I visited my friend in Brazil.*

> *I waited until I was sixteen to begin my career of stealing my dad's motor boat.*

> *I was always the fastest runner in school, clear through my freshman year. I lapped other kids. I could run faster wearing flip flops than the next fastest runner in school. And then I joined my high school track team and found out, by way of losing, how small my school was and how fast other kids in the world can run.*

Develop the Middle Part of the Essay

Once you've set the scene with your story moment, you need to offer some context and background information. The conclusion, which we'll focus on in the next chapter, will explain why the story matters. The middle part of your story is the bridge between the story action and the conclusion. That's where you fill in any blanks of information that the reader might need to know. Sometimes you don't need more than a few words or a sentence, but giving appropriate context will allow readers to understand the situation.

 For example, if you begin an essay with the swoosh of a basketball winning the Varsity Championship, then you'll need to backtrack a little and explain that after eight years of camps, conditioning, and weekend practice, you'd finally made the Varsity team. After giving this context you can then go on to conclude why this experience mattered to your life.

Let's practice on a real essay. In the following example, the student begins the story with an image. It's still dark outside, early in the morning, and it's summertime. Why isn't she still in bed like other teenagers? After setting that scene, she goes on to give the background information so that you understand that she is trying to improve her golf game.

> "The middle part of your story is the bridge between the story action and the conclusion."

I'm going to use two different colors so that you can visually see where the writer transitions from the attention-grabbing introduction to the middle part of the essay, where she gives the background information. (In the next chapter I'll show you the complete essay with its conclusion so that you can see its full progression).

The Story
(What Happened)

It was dark outside when the car pulled out of the driveway. It was summer, and I was supposed to be sleeping in, like all of my friends. But instead, I was out on the green with my Grandpa. I was willing to do anything to get my score down. The year before I had walked onto the golf team, and they had agreed to let me practice with them, but my scores weren't competitive enough to participate in the tournaments. Deep down, I wondered if they could ever be. After spending an entire season, basically on the bench, I had tried to accept that I would never be a good golfer. However, there was something inside of me that needed to find out. So long days at the driving range became my priority that summer. I remember the moment I finally connected perfectly; the ball sailed through the air. I had done it.

Background
Context
(Why It's
Happening)

Notice how the writer first sets the scene, and then goes on to explain her background with golf and her overall goals.

Write Your Rough Draft

Sit down and write out a rough draft of your story! Remember to add detail. Think about your senses: sight, smell, taste, touch and sound. Don't use ALL five senses, just pick out one or two details that will paint the clearest picture for your reader. At this point, don't worry about tying the story up with a neat bow, we'll nail the ending in the next chapter. Also, don't worry too much about spelling, editing, font, or word count. Just tell your story as though you're reporting it to a group of close friends as you sit around a fire waiting for your marshmallows to cook. Tell your story with all the anger, sadness, or hilarity you experienced when living through it, and then bridge the action part of your story and give it some background context. Explain where and how the event happened, filling in any missing information needed so that the story will make sense.

Write your own ACTION sentences:

STEP FIVE

How to End the Essay

We're getting there. In this section I'll explain the principles of how to conclude, offering lots of examples along the way. For some, the extra examples help teach the writing principle and inspire imagination. For others, the process can start to feel overwhelming and you might start to worry your own ideas aren't as good. I remember reading some of my friends' essays while I was trying to write mine, and it nearly crippled my confidence. I felt like my essays should be more like theirs, or that they were more creative, more articulate, more everything. Surprise! I got into college too. But if you're one to compare and worry, don't feel pressure to study out every single example. Just absorb the principle and then get busy working on your own conclusion.

✓ Decide What Quality You Want to Showcase

✓ Become the Ideal Candidate

✓ Practice Identifying the Concluding Point

✓ Realize that Your Conclusion Isn't the End of Your Life Story

✓ Write Out Your Conclusion

Decide What Quality You Want to Showcase

No matter how grizzly, funny, or tragic your story is, **your essay needs to end by explaining what you learned from the experience and how that made you awesome.** The ending explains why you are a complete stud muffin, and why they should definitely choose you. Only... you can't come right out and say that directly. It sounds too cocky, and just a little bossy. You can't say, *in conclusion, I am an academic magician and will make a great addition to your college.*

 Instead, you need to highlight one specific quality. Maybe your essay will show your bravery, work ethic, compassion, or your sense of humor. Your story could show your willingness to be flexible, your positive attitude, your obsession with microscopes, your passion for reading, or your natural aptitude for Algebra. So, before you start writing out your story, take a look at your list of topics and ask yourself: *What does this story teach about me and my life?* Other questions I tell my students to answer include: *What did you learn in that moment or what changed inside of me? What am I now capable of?* Ask yourself questions about the moment you have chosen to write about. What makes that moment significant?

Let's review some examples of how to further narrow down your story moment in order to capture your concluding point:

> **Topic**—*Getting cut from the high school basketball team during junior year*
> **Story Moment**—*The first day of basketball practice after being cut*
> **Concluding Point-** *?*

The essay could veer off in many directions to conclude. The focus could be on how the student showed good sportsmanship and supported his former teammates by calling them up after practice and graciously asking how things went. Or the student could spend the afternoon practicing basketball to improve his game for the next year, so as to continue developing the skill. The student might also write about spending that afternoon applying for jobs, determining that not making the team might be a new opportunity to get a part-time job and save money for college.

Each possible concluding idea could work, but the student ended up choosing to get a part-time job. So, an essay that began with his grief over being cut from the high school basketball team ended by showcasing his determination to embrace new opportunities and pursue a fresh start.

Become the Ideal Candidate

As you're trying to decide what quality to highlight in your conclusion, be aware of how you'll come across to the admissions committee. Your story should show that you're a good fit for the college, that you're an amazing student, or that you possess unique qualities. The whole point of the essay is for you to sell yourself in your own words and way. So, become their ideal candidate.

It's not enough to say, *"After crashing eighteen different motorcycles, I learned to be brave."* What the admissions committee is actually thinking is that after eighteen different crashes, you must be a door knob. A better idea would be to focus on outcomes that are admirable in a college setting. Continuing to practice motorcycle stunts despite eighteen crashes can show determination (students need that) or resilience (yep, they need that too). Explain how while multiple motorcycle crashes might appear foolish, you were determined to get back on the horse and master the motorcycle stunt. The goal is to tap into universal qualities, character traits, and outcomes that will translate well into a successful college experience.

Here are two examples of conclusions that effectively showcase something learned or an admirable quality that the student possesses. The first example shows how a childhood injury and unpleasant memories of surgeries and hospitalizations were character building. Even though enduring medical surgeries seems completely unrelated to going to college, the student's conclusion is that he is tough! He can patiently endure hard things. Those are great qualities for a college student.

By the fifth surgery I'd learned to download my own movies in advance, to pack my favorite snacks, and to avoid estimating how much school I'd miss. I couldn't un-fall from the tree, but I could go forward a little better prepared, a little more accepting that accidents happen and life goes on, and a little stronger in the knowledge that what's inside of me has patience and grit and is a whole lot tougher than my external circumstances.

The next essay uses a funny story about a childhood ear wax fetish to draw conclusions about the student's early predilection for science and research. I know the thought of ear wax is cringe-worthy, but I love how the student uses the story to show his love for science and research, definitely qualities that appeal to an admissions committee.

When my mom found out about my ear wax collection she was concerned, and she should have been concerned. It was gross, and probably not the most sustainable collection, as the lumps of ear wax were starting to dry into little piles of waxy dust. But instead of freaking out, my mom understood what I was too young to explain for myself. It was science. My creepy, childhood fixation with earwax was actually a youthful fascination with science, and the microscope I received for my birthday, along with an official science kit (petri dishes and all) transformed something a little weird and unseemly into a legitimate hobby, college major, and career path.

This final example is based on an application essay to culinary school, and while the essay began with a brief story about a dying grandmother, the conclusion answers the question of why the student wants to attend culinary school, while simultaneously showing the student in a positive way:

Although my grandma is gone I still have her recipe box, and while cooking, I bring a little bit of her life back into my own. So my desire to attend culinary school isn't limited to my passion for food, but it is also an extension of my grandmother's legacy. It's a torch I'm honored to carry.

Practice Identifying the Concluding Point

The goal is for you to successfully analyze the story moment in your essay and determine which concluding point you want to highlight. Remember, it needs to be something positive that shows you're a good fit for the college, or at least that you'd make a great student.

Let's review some essays from start to finish and see how students move from storytelling mode to the concluding point. We'll begin with the rare disease essay that we analyzed in an earlier chapter. This story starts out as a tragedy, and yet look how the student concludes by telling a story of determination and self-respect.

Topic- *Childhood medical diagnosis*
Story moment- *The moment of diagnosis*
Concluding Point- *The disease will not define the student's life or her potential*

Growing up, I was always told, like every other child, that I was special, one in a million. When I was 8 years old, I learned that I am special, but not one in a million. I am one in 25,000 diagnosed with Pseudoxanthoma Elasticum. As a third grader, I learned I would never look like other girls, and that it was likely I could lose my eyesight and suffer from heart problems. However, my diagnosis brought hardships beyond my health. Because of this disease, I have calcium deposits on my neck and chest. It looks similar to a bad rash. I was very self-conscious. I felt like people wouldn't look at my face because their eyes were busy lingering on my deformity. I didn't want to address the subject and draw attention to it, so I began retreating further and further into myself. It was in 7th grade that I made a decision: my genetic disorder is nothing more than a little bump in the road. It does not define me; it is not who I am. I am grateful that I have PXE, because it has taught me to be thankful for the present. I didn't know if one day I would wake up blind. It taught me to love myself and the body I've been blessed with. I will always have PXE, but I will never again suffer from it.

Notice the student's growth in the next essay. She begins the story as the new girl. She is scared. But as you read the essay, pay attention to the change that occurs, and how she ends by showcasing her leadership abilities.

Topic- *The new girl on the block tries out for Orchestra*
Story Moment- *The audition*
Concluding Point- *Despite being new, the student had talents to offer and leadership abilities*

It was the first day of high school orchestra, and I was terrified. I didn't know anyone. We had to perform a playing test to determine our seats, and I felt sick. Playing in front of strangers only made it worse. When it was my turn, thankfully my years of practice took over, and I let my fingers fly. Afterward, as my teacher sat me in first chair, I was completely stunned, excited, and something clicked inside me. I wasn't the uneasy girl in the back! I was the leader of an entire section. I realized I could do this, and I warmly introduced myself to the other cellists and eventually, the rest of the orchestra. Over time as I grew into a leader, I met many great people, and learned that my circle of friends could be as big as I wanted.

This next essay also focuses on one specific moment when a student is at church feeling homesick and inept. And yet as the story continues, she demonstrates how she was able to overcome an obstacle by going for it, and how that boost of confidence helped her overcome the trial of homesickness.

Topic- *Overcoming homesickness as a Choir Director*
Story Moment- *The first choir performance*
Concluding Point- *The student showed courage and gained confidence by trying something new (leading music)*

Most people feel the spirit during the sacrament meeting hymns, but all I felt was homesick. The whispers of the congregation combined with the pounding of the organ were too harsh. My new congregation may have been indifferent to music, but music had always been important to me and I wanted to help. I presented to the bishop the benefits of a church choir. They hadn't had one in years, but he loved the idea, and my Mom and I were soon invited to be choir directors. I had never led music before, but I was willing. Our first performance was just shy of a miracle. Somehow, we filled all the choir seats and pulled off our song. As the final notes of the piano rang, I gestured the choir to sit. I felt a sense of peace washing over me, suddenly realizing I didn't feel so far from home anymore.

Realize that Your Conclusion Isn't the End of Your Life Story

The end of your essay is not necessarily the official end of your story. You don't need to say, "and at the end of the summer, my grandma died" or "it took six more months for my wrists to heal completely" or "I never rode a motorcycle again." How your story ends, the punch line, matters much less than what you learned through that experience. Let me say that a different way: **Your story needs to suck them in and entertain them just long enough for you to show your positive growth.**

In the following example, the student writes about how her dad's employment situation created instability at home. Notice that she doesn't conclude by tying up her home life with a pretty bow. Those details don't matter to the story. Instead, after establishing the situation she moves the discussion to how this experience affected her attitude:

Up until I was 15, my home life had always been stable. I remember the day when my Dad told us he had just taken a job in Northern California. Due to the logistics of the move, our family decided to stay in Chicago while he travelled back and forth during the workweek. While my Mom juggled parenting four kids alone, as the oldest, I quickly became the one she could rely on. On top of my homework, sports and extracurriculars, I now had to help run the family as well. The instability spiraled as my dad lost his job my junior year and was unemployed for over seven months. He finally received a job offer, but it would require our family to move to Southern California. We had no other choice than to take it. The first two months of my senior year we were living in Airbnb's because we couldn't find a house in time for school to start. When I sat down to take the ACT, I didn't even know what address to write on the form. What I learned from this experience was that stability isn't based on the situation, but in how I choose to react. Despite this very difficult time, I was able to maintain my grade, and keep a positive attitude, striving to embrace the beach even on days when I missed the snow and rain.

Write Your Conclusion

Now that you have a rough draft of your story, read back through it and identify what you learned that day, or how you changed, or what positive quality you developed. What specifically are you going to tell the admissions committee about yourself? Once you have a goal in mind, like how you want to showcase your unique foreign language abilities, or how you can multi-task, or how you can appropriately deal with stress, try writing your conclusion. Remember, don't club them over the head with it in a cocky, bossy way. Just cue the music, raise the lights, and go for your Kumbaya Ah-Ha moment!

Qualities you'd like to showcase:

STEP SIX

Revising, Editing, & Making it Look Good

This is the hardest part. You have a great topic, you've narrowed it to a great story moment, and you're looking at a rough draft that finishes with your concluding point. Only... it's not quite right. Here's what you can do:

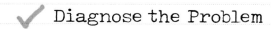 **Diagnose the Problem**

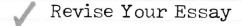 **Revise Your Essay**

✓ **Get Outside Help**

Diagnose the Problem

First, let me speak to those who are curled in the fetal position with a crumpled essay in one fist. Take a deep breath. There are many ways to get help with your essay, but you are the most important editor, so I want to begin with some simple things that you can do. Later, I'll address reaching out to others for help with your essay.

We need to diagnose whether it's the topic that's the problem, meaning the story you've chosen to tell and the subsequent concluding point, or if it's the actual writing that is suffering. Even if your topic seems amazing, if the story is boring and the conclusion is failing to deliver a specific insight into your awesomeness, you may need to start over. I know. I'm the worst. It's possible that with enough work you can pass off a boring topic as an excellent college essay, and I, for one, would love that challenge. But, I'm operating under the assumption that you're not a professional writer and do not want to

> "Even if your topic seems amazing, if the story is boring and the conclusion is failing to deliver a specific insight into your awesomeness, you may need to start over."

spend every minute for the next month squeezing water out of a rock. Just try again, and make sure that you understand what story you're trying to tell and what quality you're trying to showcase.

Revise Your Essay

If your essay topic is working, but the writing is lousy, let's fix it. I've provided a list of revision steps below to strengthen the quality of your essay. It works best if you focus on each one in order:

1. BREAK THE STORY DOWN INTO PARTS

You need to make sure all the parts of your essay are there, regardless of the word count. We'll get to that later. First, **what happened?** Begin in the middle of the action, whether you're tripping, lost, holding your dying grandmother's hand, or showing up during your teacher's office hours to get extra help. This is the moment where you describe what is happening in a way that will practically force the admissions committee to stop yawning and pay attention.

Second, **why is this event happening?** Were you running in a regional track meet when you tripped? Were you flunking Calculus when you decided to get help every day during your lunch period? Are you the new kid on the block after sixteen moves, or did you mow lawns for six months to save money for your trip? Briefly explain the circumstances surrounding your story.

Finally, offer explanation and insight as to **why this experience matters** or what you learned, and how that has affected your character. The key here is to use your story to answer the question asked in the essay prompt, and to show the admissions committee what you're made of. You need to be clear in your own mind about what question you're answering and what positive attribute you're trying to showcase. If you're confused about this, re-read chapter five.

In the following two examples I have highlighted with color the different parts of the essay.

It was dark outside when the car pulled out of the driveway. It was summer, and I was supposed to be sleeping in like all of my friends. But instead, I was out on the green with my Grandpa. I was willing to do anything to get my score down. The year before I had walked onto the golf team, and they had agreed to let me practice with them, but my scores weren't competitive enough to participate in the tournaments. Deep down, I wondered if they ever could be. After spending an entire season basically on the bench, I had tried to accept that I would never be a good golfer. However, there was something inside of me that needed to find out. So long days at the driving range became my priority that summer. I remember the moment I finally connected perfectly; the ball sailed through the air. I had done it. This experience helped me realize that I don't need to be confined to a limited view of myself, and sometimes, the only thing that holds me back is my fear of failing. When I get out of my own head, I try harder, do better, and accomplish so much more. This quality will be crucial to my academic success. My experience with golf has taught me to stop defining myself by what I can and can't do, and to instead focus on what I might be able to do if I try.

The Story
(What Happened)

Background Context
(Why It's Happening)

Concluding Point
(Why It Matters)

In this second example, notice how the context (the blue font) is couched in the middle of the story. You don't have to marry yourself to a high-maintenance, color coded order. Just make sure all the parts are there.

The Story
(What Happened)

Background
Context
(Why It's
Happening)

Concluding
Point
(Why It
Matters)

As I sat in the plush chair in the House Chamber, I wanted to sink through it and melt into the floor. My high school Youth and Government Club had been invited to a debate in the Springfield, Illinois state capitol building. My opponent was viciously calling me out on everything I believed in and trying to disprove my points. I didn't feel like the composed representative I was supposed to be. After we went back to the hotel that night, I sat on my bed and went over the arguments of the day. As I thought about it all, I kept coming back to the representative that so vehemently disagreed with me. I mulled over his point of view and what made him think the way he did. As I contemplated, I gradually began to understand his side of the issue. I'm so grateful for that experience, because learning to appreciate the opposing view allowed my own political views to blossom, and surprisingly enabled me to argue more effectively. I realized I could maintain my own values, but still be understanding. Since then, I've been an eager student of government, politics, and current events. Now, living in Southern California, I often meet people with varying backgrounds and opinions, but it no longer makes me feel vulnerable. I have gained confidence in expressing myself while remaining a respectful listener, and I feel that this quality will be critical to engage with other students and work together towards common goals.

Now look your essay over as a whole. Did you tell the story well, offer the necessary background or contextual information, and then finally showcase something about yourself? That wasn't a philosophical question, it was an actual question. **Make sure all the parts of the essay are there.**

2. ADD INTERESTING DETAIL

A quick way to write a good essay is to write a story as if you're telling it to a crowd of eager listeners. Embellish, give details, make those mamas cry. If you're writing about falling out of a tree, I want to hear how those wrist bones crunched on impact. If you're writing about putting down the family dog, I want to know the final words that you whispered into Rover's ear. And if your story is about how you once got lost in Tijuana, Mexico, I'd better smell nachos! Sensory details in the form of blood, guts, ear wax, or homemade soup will bring the story to life. People are lured in and curious about personal details. We can't help ourselves. So, although the required word count might limit your ability to embellish the story, do your best to tell it in interesting ways in the space allotted.

If you're struggling to find the right details, try slowing the story down. Instead of writing *I fell out of a tree in my backyard*, try describing how it felt to be flying through the air. What was your body doing? How did you feel inside? What did the situation look like? What were you worried about? Slowing down and offering lots of details about a specific moment in your story can help provide a stronger frame to make the story stand taller.

Here are two examples of slowing down the story:

If you're writing about a motorcycle accident, the speed of your motorcycle, the weather conditions, and the feel of the wind on your helmetless head are all interesting and relevant details.

If you're writing about how you learned to love books by reading Harry Potter aloud to your work-weary, medical student dad, the details about his grueling hospital schedule, your tender young age, and the fluffy blanket you tucked around him all paint a loving, resonant image of how books bring people together, how stories soothe and comfort.

Ask yourself, what kind of story am I telling, and what kind of details will people be interested in reading? If your story involves soup, I want to know if it's borscht or your grandma's cheesy potato chowder. If your story is about pimple popping, I want to know...I don't want to know but I HAVE to know, how much puss are we talking? Don't shy away from making your story come alive with real, pertinent, cringe-worthy detail.

3. AVOID OVERLY FORMAL OR FANCY LANGUAGE

The best student essays sound like they were written by normal teenagers., not students practicing their vocabulary words for the SAT. I have a painful cautionary tale to exemplify this principle.

As a sophomore in high school, I was invited to apply for a spot in an Honors English class. We were expected to write our way into this particular course, and I really wanted in, so I took drastic measures to ensure that my essay sounded mature. During study hall one morning, which happened to take place in the same classroom that also held the coveted Honors class, I suddenly noticed a list of Latin root words tacked to the board. In a flash of inspiration, I decided to spruce up my application essay with some fancy vocabulary. After all, the teacher in charge of the Honors class had created that list of words...these were her words, so, she must be partial to them, right? I just knew she'd be impressed if I integrated them into my essay.

Unfortunately for me, the Latin root posted to the board was "circum" and all the subsequent vocabulary words included the root "circum." Undeterred, I included the words circumvent, circumnavigate, and circumspect all in one short essay. To this day I cannot imagine what that teacher must've thought. Oh, and I didn't get into the Honors class.

I'm assuming that most of you won't cram your essays full of weird words based on a shared Latin root. But many students try to make their writing sound "professor-ish." The problem is that overly formal language feels disingenuous to read. Or overly dramatic. Look at the difference between these two sentences:

Example 1- I gasped and heaved in unmitigated despair and choked on the storm of tears gathering in my throat as I retreated to my inner sanctuary, doomed to pass a sleepless night.

Example 2- I cried myself to sleep.

I tell my students all the time that they can be raw but keep it real. Try to dial back the gasping, heaving, and storms of tears. I'm not suggesting your first sentence be "Hey there Admissions Dawg, wuz up?" Don't be overly familiar. Just try to sound like yourself.

4. READ YOUR STORY ALOUD

Often you will hear the problems with your story, even when you can't see them as you read silently. Try reading your essay aloud. Is it too choppy? Are there sentences that run on too long? Does it flow smoothly, or do you abruptly change the subject? Are you repeating yourself? Are there tangents? Cut that stuff out. Reading aloud will help you identify problem areas. It really helps to read it aloud to someone else. Do you feel the need to stop and explain something? Is there a sentence that is confusing or hard to read? Sometimes waiting at least one day and reading it over "cold" will allow you to notice things you missed before.

Finally, ask someone else to read your essay aloud to you. Do they stumble over any sentences? Are there awkward parts? Hearing someone read it back to you allows you to become the audience and put yourself in the admission committees' shoes.

5. CUT DOWN THE WORD COUNT

When I'm tutoring students, this is where we always spend the most time. Once the story, context and concluding points are nailed down in a rough draft, we begin shaving each sentence down. Say each point once and only once and stick to what is important to the overall message. Read it again and take out some detail, leaving the best detail. Can you substitute one verb in place of a bunch of little verbs? Can you get rid of the words "really" and "very?" Read it again and shave it down a little more. Rinse, repeat. Until you achieve the specified word count. Here are some examples:

Try to take a couple of words out of each sentence.
Trim each sentence.

See what I just did? I reduced eleven words to three. Here's another example:

I really hoped to try and be able to attend the football game.
I wanted to go to the game.

Or if it's already clear that you're talking about going to a football game, you could even write:

I was desperate to go.

We went from thirteen words to five. If you trim all of your sentences that much, you can easily reduce a 500-word essay to 250 words.

When you're revising for word count, you have to keep reading and re-reading, taking out whatever extra words that you can, or rephrasing it in a simpler way. This is crucial for short answer "essays." In the following examples, students were asked to list several of their extracurricular activities or work experiences, and then write a brief description. Basically, these are mini essays and the word count is brutal, but **they all achieve a story and convey a positive attribute:**

> ***Seven years of playing cello:*** *My heart raced as the tempo surged. But I had been over this section countless times, and I was ready. From sixth grade, when I had to lug my cello to school and home, to senior year, it all led here. I have been able to utilize my talent at recitals, concerts, retirement homes, and church services. I have discovered that music is a powerful way to bear testimony; it is my ability to touch hearts.*

Volunteer Service at Feed My Starving Children: The first time I watched the opening film at Feed My Starving Children, I felt my heartstrings pull. As I put on the hairnet and washed my hands, I pictured the children's hopeful faces. This was the first time I passionately took up a cause. I loaded the rice, soy, protein, and vegetables, and sent them to be sealed and packed into boxes, knowing with each bag I was helping to feed a starving child.

Bakery Employment: It was late when my shift ended, and I mentally reviewed my to-do list. I had a test the next day, and I had exactly enough time left before bed to study. Before I started working at the bakery, I struggled to finish everything and get to bed at a decent hour. Surprisingly, working forced me to manage my time more efficiently. This is a skill that will follow me into college and, eventually, my career. Balancing is not an act, but a calculated, purposeful decision.

6. PERFORM SPELL CHECK

It's weird that I have to remind students to do this, but there you are. Here are two examples from real papers written by college kids who would've done well to use spell check:

> *As I reached for his hand, I felt the excrement rise within me.*
> *More and more people are shopping at discount whorehouses.*

Spell check it. Make sure to read and double-check the suggested replacement words. And if you revise it or change something, spell check again!

Getting Outside Help

One of the best things you can do is to have other people read your essays and give you feedback. One of the worst things you can do is...have other people read your essays and give you feedback. Obviously, this presents a problem. So let's talk about how to go about revising and editing in a way that will help you, instead of leaving you binge drinking Coke and Pop Rocks, having sworn off college forever.

First of all, be cautious when dealing with helpful parents. I can't say this loudly enough, although I truly don't want to hurt feelings. While some parent advice improves the experience, many times it becomes a "too many cooks in the kitchen" situation. I don't care if they graduated from the University of Whatever, Summa Cum Whatever. If your parent is desperate to help, invite them to go through the steps of this book with you so that you're all on the same page. Having said that, I'm all about soliciting parent feedback on possible writing topics or nailing down the best concluding angle for your essay.

> "The whole point of this book is that it's a crucial life skill to know where to go when you need help."

If you need more help revising, ask for suggestions from your school writing center (if there is one), your English teacher, or your guidance counselor. One of them should know how to connect you with the help that you need. The whole point of this book is that it's a crucial life skill to know where to go when you need help. So, if the help you need is line-by-line editing, go directly to a capable source!

Form, Guidelines, and Due Dates

A few years ago, I worked with a student who had a natural penchant for writing. She wrote stories and poetry, and I wondered if she'd been binge watching the movie *Legally Blonde* because she was definitely more excited to tackle her college essay than most. Not surprisingly, the rough draft of her essay was an extremely creative, off-roading foray into free form poetry. The English Teacher side of me was pleased with her innovative work. The College Essay Tutor side of me gave a deep sigh. Free form poetry doesn't easily translate in the college application setting. Maybe it could, but it would require the perfect chemistry between the student and the admissions committee. No matter how talented you are, you'd need to appeal to their poetry sensibilities in exactly the right way, with fingers crossed. In my professional opinion, the gamble is too great.

The creativity and individuality of your work, not the form of it, should make your essay stand out. For many admissions committees, the act of bucking their form specifications, even in the name of creativity, *feels* cheeky. Maybe there are a handful out there in the world who might love your poetry and love you. But the chances of it working out are risky. I started this book by encouraging you to get online and research all the application essay requirements for the colleges you're applying to. I can't emphasize enough that *it shows respect and maturity to follow all of their specifications.* Write an essay, not a journal entry, short story, or Haiku. Pay attention to font, word count, and due dates.

Don't make the rookie mistake and assume that readers won't notice you filled the white space with size 18 font.

I have worked with many students who felt casual about some of these guidelines, and I'm always quick to correct them. Your future education is at the mercy of these schools, so pay attention to details and **take all of the guidelines seriously**.

Helpful contact information:

Name:
Phone:
Email:

Name:
Phone:
Email:

Name:
Phone:
Email:

Name:
Phone:
Email:

Name:
Phone:
Email:

Name:
Phone:
Email:

Name:
Phone:
Email:

(local college advisors, writing centers, helpful friends, etc.)

Conclusion

The six-step process that I outlined in this book gives you boulders to help you cross the rapids. I laid out the path, now it's your job to jump from rock to rock. Mostly, I want to encourage you. It's been my privilege over the years to help men, women, rich kids, poor kids, funny kids, weird kids and international students. I've also helped many mature adults who were returning to school or reinventing their careers. The single factor that matters is your willingness to work. You need to want it and be hungry for it. When I've read stacks and stacks of essays, I can tell a mile away which students really stuck their neck out and tried, no matter their natural writing abilities. I've read boring, lazy essays written by gifted writers, and I've read amazing essays that were awkwardly and haltingly drafted by non-writers. The only down side to witnessing students bravely stick their neck out by applying to college is to occasionally see someone with enormous potential slap together a "good enough" essay and turn it in unfinished.

Years ago, when interviewing the head of admissions at BYU, I asked him how much the committee weights the essays. How much do they even matter? He explained that there is a small percentage of genius savants who automatically get accepted based on their Albert Einstein numbers. Conversely, there is a larger number that are flat out rejected due to their low scores and grade point averages. However, the bulk of student applications are somewhere in the middle. Since their test scores and grades didn't distinguish them, for better or worse, it's the uniqueness of their circumstances, life experiences, and personality that are taken into consideration. That's the essay portion, folks! **If an Admissions Committee is on the fence about you, it's probably your essay that will determine their answer.** And even if you haven't cured cancer yet or grown up in an African orphanage, your experiences and personality can leap off the page in a memorable way. It's all about telling them a good story. Like I said before, make sure that while they're sitting on the couch munching on Cheetos after work, they're shaking their head or chuckling as they remember your essay.

The process may be tedious, but the possibilities are endless. Many of my students have recycled their essays later on in life, as they've applied for graduate programs, scholarships, and study abroad opportunities. So, get as much mileage out of this process as you can. Today is your day. **Get up off the couch, sit down at your computer, and write your way in!**

About the Author

Lauren Gillespie started out at *The American University of Paris*, but later transferred to *Brigham Young University* where she received a Bachelor's in English and a Master's degrees in American Literature and Folklore. She lives in Naperville, IL with her husband and four children.

Made in United States
North Haven, CT
14 September 2022

24106741R30035